SUPERSTARS OF SPORTS

# KRIS BRYANT

## BASEBALL SUPERSTAR

BY TYLER OMOTH

D1306791

**CAPSTONE PRESS**
a capstone imprint

Blazers Books are published by Capstone Press,
1710 Roe Crest Drive, North Mankato, Minnesota 56003
www.mycapstone.com

**Library of Congress Cataloging-in-Publication Data**
Names: Omoth, Tyler author.
Title: Kris Bryant : baseball superstar / by Tyler Omoth.
Description: North Mankato, Minnesota : An imprint of Capstone Press, [2019]
  | Series: Blazers. Superstars of Sports | Includes index. | Audience:
  Ages: 9-14.
Identifiers: LCCN 2018002676 (print) | LCCN 2018005151 (ebook) | ISBN
  9781543525144 (eBook PDF) | ISBN 9781543525069 (hardcover) | ISBN
  9781543525106 (paperback)
Subjects: LCSH: Bryant, Kris, 1992- Juvenile literature. | Baseball
  players—United States—Biography—Juvenile literature. | Chicago Cubs
  (Baseball team)—History—Juvenile literature.
Classification: LCC GV865.B796 (ebook) | LCC GV865.B796 O56 2019 (print)
LC record available at https://lccn.loc.gov/2018002676

**Editorial Credits**
Carrie Braulick Sheely, editor; Kyle Grenz, designer; Eric Gohl, media researcher;
Tori Abraham, production specialist

**Photo Credits**
AP Photo: Four Seam Images/Tony Farlow, 17, Lenny Ignelzi, 13, 14; Getty Images: Brace
Hemmelgarn, 8, Ethan Miller, 7, Icon Sportswire, 26, Joe Robbins, 5, Mike McGinnis, 18, Stacy
Revere, 29; Newscom: Icon SMI/Josh Holmberg, 11, Icon Sportswire/Frank Jansky, 20, Icon
Sportswire/Roy K. Miller, 6, Icon Sportswire/Warren Wimmer, 25, TNS/Chris Sweda, 21, UPI/
Brian Kersey, 23, USA Today Sports/Winslow Townson, cover

Design Elements: Shutterstock

**Quote Sources**
Page 9, "Bryant says he'll do whatever Cubs ask of him." 12 July 2013. DailyHerald.com. http://
www.dailyherald.com/article/20130712/sports/707129681/
Page 10, "Kris Bryant the one who got away from Blue Jays." 14 July 2015. Sportsnet. https://
www.sportsnet.ca/baseball/mlb/kris-bryant-the-one-that-got-away-from-blue-jays/
Page 15, "Sky is the limit for college slugger Bryant." 12 May 2013. MLB.com. https://www.
mlb.com/news/university-of-san-diego-third-baseman-kris-bryant-likely-top-10-pick-in-
draft/c-47315710
Page 22, "Joe Maddon on Kris Bryant: He's only about winning."30 September 2015. ESPN.
http://www.espn.com/blog/chicago/cubs/post/_/id/34680/joe-maddon-on-kris-bryant-hes-
only-about-winning
Page 28, "How Kris Bryant topped his MVP season with Cubs." 01 October 2017. NBC Sports.
http://www.nbcsports.com/chicago/chicago-cubs/how-kris-bryant-topped-his-mvp-season-
cubs-nl-mvp-rendon-arenado-votto-stanton

Printed and bound in the United States of America.
PA017

# TABLE OF CONTENTS

# CHAPTER 1

# MAKING OF A STAR

Kris Bryant got ready to bat on June 27, 2016. He smashed a home run! The crowd cheered. He became the first Major League Baseball (MLB) player to hit three home runs and two **doubles** in a game.

**double**—when a player hits the ball and reaches second base without the help of an error or trying to put out another runner

Kris became the youngest player in Cubs history to hit three home runs in a game on June 27, 2016. He was 24 years old.

Kris smashes his third home run on June 27, 2016.

Kris was born in Las Vegas, Nevada, on January 4, 1992. His parents are Mike and Susie Bryant. He also has an older brother, Nick.

**minor league**—a league of teams where players improve their playing skills before joining a major-league team

Kris' father started playing for the Boston Red Sox in 1980. He played two years in the team's **minor leagues**.

Kris hugs his father during an MLB event in 2015.

*"It's been awesome to have him as a dad. He's kind of taught me the way to go about my journey . . ."*
—Kris Bryant

Mike Bryant taught his sons how to hit baseballs in a **batting cage** at the family home. Mike also coached Kris' **Little League** team. When Kris was 12, his team went to the state tournament.

**batting cage**—a structure used to practice hitting baseballs; baseballs come out of a machine for batters to hit and a net catches the balls

**Little League**—an international baseball league for children

*"You learn to grow up, you learn a lot of things in college that you don't know when you're in high school. I'm really glad I got to experience that."*

—Kris Bryant

Kris played shortstop at Bonanza High School in Las Vegas. He was known for hitting towering home runs. The Toronto Blue Jays **drafted** him in 2010. Kris chose to go to college instead of playing in the minor leagues.

**draft**—to select a player to join a sports organization or team

In 2010 Kris won a *USA Today* Baseball Player of the Year award.

Kris gets ready to bat for Bonanza High School in a 2010 game.

# CHAPTER 2

# COLLEGE BALL

Kris went to the University of San Diego (USD). He played third base for the Toreros. Kris was a **starter** as a **freshman**. His hitting skill quickly made him a star player. In his first season he had a batting average (BA) of .365.

**starter**—a player who takes a position at the beginning of a game

**freshman**—a person in his or her first year of college

Kris planned on being a dentist if he couldn't become a pro baseball player.

Kris gets ready to throw the ball in a game against the University of Santa Barbara in 2013.

Kris hit more home runs in 2013 than entire teams did. He had more home runs than 223 teams in his *division*.

Kris connects for a home run in a 2013 game.

*"Sky's the limit. You don't like to put expectations on kids. But I'll tell you I've never coached a guy like him."*

—Rich Hill, USD baseball coach

In the 2013 season, Kris crushed 31 home runs. He won the Golden Spikes Award. This award is given to the best **amateur** baseball player in the United States each year.

**division**—a small group of teams that compete against one another

**amateur**—an athlete who is not paid for playing a sport

# CHAPTER 3

# WELCOME TO THE PROS

The Chicago Cubs drafted Kris in 2013. In 2014 he started playing with the Tennessee Smokies minor-league team. Kris was named an **all-star**. He also won the Southern League Home Run **Derby**.

**all-star**—an honor given to the best players at each position in a league

**derby**—a contest

Kris accepts the award for winning the Southern League Home Run Derby in 2014.

Kris celebrates after hitting his first MLB home run in Milwaukee, Wisconsin.

In 2015 Kris was ready for the major-league team. He became the Cubs' starting third baseman. Kris didn't hit a home run in his first 91 tries. But after his first homer in May, he kept launching them.

Kris hits a single during Game 2 of the 2016 World Series.

In 2016 the Cubs won 103 games.

They went to the World Series.

In Game 7 Kris scored two runs.

He also made the final out of the series.

Kris' great play helped the Cubs win

the championship.

Kris (center) celebrates with teammates after winning the 2016 World Series.

FACT

Before 2016 the Cubs had not been to the World Series since 1945. A curse is said to have started that year. Some people said it kept the Cubs from winning the World Series.

Kris helped the Cubs have another great season in 2017. They became the division champions and played in the National League (NL) Championship Series. Kris ended the season with a BA of .295.

*"This guy is focused every day."*
—Joe Maddon, Cubs manager

Kris hits a single during a 2017 game against the Los Angeles Dodgers.

# CHAPTER 4

# CAREER HIGHLIGHTS

Kris has already won many awards in his MLB career. He won the NL **Rookie** of the Year award in 2015. His BA was .275 with 99 runs batted in (RBI) and 26 home runs. He received every vote for the award.

**rookie**—a first-year player

Kris advances to third base after hitting a triple in a game against the Pittsburgh Pirates in 2015.

Kris receives the National League MVP award for the 2016 season.

In 2016 Kris improved even more. His BA was .292 with 39 home runs and 102 RBIs. He was named the NL Most Valuable Player (MVP).

FACT

Kris won the Rookie of the Year and the MVP award in back-to-back seasons. Only three other players have done that.

Kris is the first Cubs player in history to play in 150 games in each of his first three years.

Kris has enjoyed his success, but he stays focused. He continues to try to improve. He works hard to stay healthy. Fans look forward to what the future holds for one of MLB's brightest stars.

*"You just stay where you are, stay in the moment and enjoy it. Play hard, but don't really worry about the future too much."*

—Kris Bryant

Kris signs autographs for fans in Milwaukee, Wisconsin, before a game.

# TIMELINE

**-1992-**
Kristopher Lee Bryant is born in Las Vegas, Nevada.

**-2011-**
Kris is named a Freshman All-American and a West Coast Conference Co-Freshman and Co-Player of the Year.

**-2010-**
Kris is named to the *USA Today* All-USA high school baseball team.

The Toronto Blue Jays draft Kris, but he does not sign.

# GLOSSARY

**all-star** (OL-star)—an honor given to the best players at each position in a league

**amateur** (AM-uh-chur)—an athlete who is not paid for playing a sport

**batting cage** (BAT-ing KAYJ)—a structure used to practice hitting baseballs; baseballs come out of a machine for batters to hit and a net catches the balls

**derby** (DUR-bee)—a contest

**division** (di-VIZH-uhn)—a small group of teams in a conference that compete against one another; divisions are often grouped by location

**double** (DUH-buhl)—when a player hits the ball and reaches second base without the help of an error or attempt to put out another runner

**draft** (DRAFT)—to select a player to join a sports organization or team

**freshman** (FRESH-muhn)—a person in his or her first year of college

**minor league** (MYE-nur LEEG)—a league of teams where players improve their skills before joining a major-league team

**rookie** (RUK-ee)—a first-year player

**starter** (START-ur)—a player who appears in games when they start

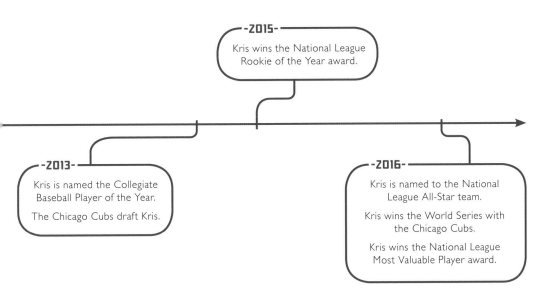

-2015-
Kris wins the National League Rookie of the Year award.

-2013-
Kris is named the Collegiate Baseball Player of the Year.

The Chicago Cubs draft Kris.

-2016-
Kris is named to the National League All-Star team.

Kris wins the World Series with the Chicago Cubs.

Kris wins the National League Most Valuable Player award.

# READ MORE

**Fishman, Jon M.** *Kris Bryant.* Sports All-Stars. Minneapolis: Lerner Publications, 2018.

**Gitlin, Marty.** *Kris Bryant: Baseball Star.* Biggest Names in Sports. Lake Elmo, Minn.: Focus Readers, 2017.

**Storden, Thom.** *Amazing Baseball Records.* Epic Sports Records. North Mankato, Minn.: Capstone Press, 2015.

# INTERNET SITES

Use FactHound to find Internet sites related to this book.

Visit *www.facthound.com*

Just type in **9781543525069** and go.

# INDEX